Clever Cryptograms

Louise B. Moll

Illustrated by Jim Sharpe

Sterling Publishing Co., Inc.
New York

This book is dedicated to my daughter, Andrea, who is the very best part of me.

Acknowledgment
I want to thank Dr. Wesley E. Bramnick for his technical advice, and Mr. Barry L. Sherman for making his resources available.

Library of Congress Cataloging-in-Publication Data Available

10   9

Published by Sterling Publishing Co., Inc.
387 Park Avenue South, New York, NY 10016
© 1994 by Louise Moll
Illustrations © 1994 by Jim Sharpe
Distributed in Canada by Sterling Publishing
℅ Canadian Manda Group, 165 Dufferin Street,
Toronto, Ontario, Canada M6K 3H6
Distributed in Great Britain by Chrysalis Books Group PLC
The Chrysalis Building, Bramley Road, London, W10 6SP, England
Distributed in Australia by Capricorn Link (Australia) Pty. Ltd.
P.O. Box 704, Windsor, NSW 2756, Australia

Manufactured in the United States of America

Sterling ISBN 0-8069-0756-8

For information about custom editions, special sales, premium and
corporate purchases, please contact Sterling Special Sales
Department at 800-805-5489 or specialsales@sterlingpub.com.

Contents

A Note for Cryptographers

If you're a cryptogram lover, you'll know how difficult it has been to find any cryptogram collections. You solve the handful in the crossword puzzle magazines, of course, but then what? The buffs who want to settle into a cozy, long evening with pencil, eraser and enough cryptograms to last the night, are out of luck.

Finding no books available in stores or racks anywhere, I decided to put one together myself. Since it is important to find a meaningful message when you break a code, I began searching through philosophy books. What better source of material could there be than the greatest sages of all time!

The quotations in this book span the centuries and are as significant today as they were when they were written. For me, they open doors in my mind and provide food for my soul. I hope you get as much pleasure from solving them as I had in selecting and disguising them.

How to Use This Book

A cryptogram is a communication in code, using a scrambled alphabet that substitutes one letter for another. Breaking it is an exercise in logic, imagination and perseverance. Logic, as you search out the patterns and structure of the words and sentences you're trying to uncover. Imagination, as you intuit words from the jumble before you. Perseverance, as you stick with the trial and error search.

If you've never solved a cryptogram before, you'll need to know certain facts: Each cryptogram is coded differently, but in any single quotation, the code is consistent. No letter ever stands for itself.

For example, a C could represent an E throughout the message, and an F could be an R.

```
WE'RE    PUZZLED    PUZZLERS
HC'FC    KYNNACP    KYNNACFX
```

The most common three-letter words include *the, and, but, for* and *are.* Common two-letter words are *it, is, of,* and *in.* Long word endings include *ing, ion, est* and *ied.*

Start by tracking down these telltale patterns, and with the letters you detect, you'll soon clue into other formations that will eventually reveal the message.

The order of frequency of the most used letters in the English language is:

E - T - A - O - I - N - S - H - R - D - L - U

and it has probably never helped anyone to know that!

Have fun with these crypts!

St. Thomas Aquinas

(1225–1274)

1. DNHSJRZ ISJFWV RQ GJUL HWHJF
CHARITY BRINGS TO LIFE AGAIN

RNQVL KNQ HSL VCJSJRYHGGZ
THOSE WHO ARE SPIRITUALLY

TLHT.
DEAD

2. LGWBUFC UW T FCXBTUR
JUSTICE IS A CERTAIN

XCFBUBGYC KD JURY PMCXCAN T
RECTITUDE OF MIND WHEREBY A

JTR YKCW PMTB MC KGVMB BK YK
MAN DOES WHAT HE OUGHT TO DO

UR BMC FUXFGJWBTRFCW
IN THE CIRCUMSTANCES

FKRDXKRBURV MUJ.
CONFRONTING HIM

3. CQCWG OZEI KWNYXY RADYC
EVERY MIND GRASPS THOSE

RAZEKY RANR NWC ODYR MDOODE,
THINGS THAT ARE MOST COMMON

YFMA NY UCZEK, DEC, NEI KDDI.
SUCH AS BEING ONE AND GOOD

4. OIQ FW IT ZPKFTITSN ZY
LAW IS AN ORDINANCE OF

PNIWZT YZP AJN SZVVZT CZZK,
REASON FOR THE COMMON GOOD

VIKN UL JFV QJZ JIW SIPN ZY AJN
MADE BY HIM WHO HAS CARE OF THE

SZVVMTFAL.
COMMUNITY

5. ECC JSY ECNQS, PZXF MVNCXL
ALL MEN ALIVE BOTH GUILTY

EYI NYYZASYX, INS XFS ISEXF ZW
AND INNOCENT DIE THE DEATH OF

YEXVKS.
NATURE

8

W

6. SEG VQBG PB WFUIG EUZ SEG

THE LIFE OF GRACE HAS THE

YUSLFG, YPS PB UY GYH, TLS PB

NATURE NOT OF AN END BUT OF

ZPXGSEQYW SEUS QZ U XGUYZ

SOMETHING THAT IS A MEANS

SPKUFH UY GYH.

TOWARD AN END

7. KYAQA NF MU WNMB UC FNM

THERE IS NO KIND OF SIN

EYNVY NF MUK FUHAKNHAF BGA KU

WHICH IS NOT SOMETIMES DUE TO

KYA BAHUMF' FGPPAFKNUM.

THE DEMONS SUGGESTION

8. XMO MAZVP GNAU APCOBGXVPCG

THE HUMAN SOUL UNDERSTANDS

TXGOUQ XMBNAFM TXG NRP VHX

ITSELF THROUGH ITS OWN ACT

NQ APCOBGXVPCTPF, GMNRTPF

OF UNDERSTANDING SHOWING

JOBQOHXUE TXG JNROB VPC PVXABO.

PERFECTLY ITS POWER AND NATURE

9. WTZ ETZ GD NAU GCZ TEEGIL

MAN CAN OF HIS OWN ACCORD

DTSS AZMG UAZ, HRM NJ ETZZGM

FALL INTO SIN BUT HE CANNOT

TLYTZEJ MGCTILU WJIAM CAMNGRM

ADVANCE TOWARDS MERIT WITHOUT

LAYAZJ TUUAUMTZEJ.

DIVINE ASSISTANCE

10. LWFQCD ND PFD NQ LFEIWL

VNJW BCG ND EIW HCLVG.

Answers on page 102.

9

Pearl Buck

(1892–1973)

1. TG UIOFL SGNLAD FPG CUG
ELRV HPGFCIPGD TUE FPG FSRG
CE CUNLQ EB EIP ETL GLM,
TNCUEIC MEISC EP BFNCU.

2. YT C BCL GVBKI XV RV NYI VPL
SVVR TVZ HVF, XNKL BFIX HVF
TOKK XNCX BCL CLR ICEK
HVFZIKOT.

3. LRTD URT STHSZT HQ BDX
OHPDUEX ORHHWT STBOT BU BZZ
OHWUW, DHU TYTD MTDTEBZW OBD
ABVT LBE.

4. ZX ZA SQXXQG XY OQNGU
QNGOI YB XTQ ZUQJZXNSOQ
RQEXTA, BYG XTQU AYGGYK NUR
RQNXT XNPQ XTQZG EGYEQG
EONWQ ZU OZBQ, NUR YUQ ZA UYX
NBGNZR.

5. OLRZPAR TPXB, LR LW BCWD RP
HBTLBXB RZCR JBCRZ LW GLICT,
HAR OLRZ LR — LKNPWWLHTB!

6. AG KLA JAGMW MPLN LA LKUSDRLA
MDEE RGAWNSQRN MPUA PU DW LYEU
NG LCCGSV PDW GMA PGQWU.

7. NMJL GAE NTL XNHLGJ DGXX ZA.

8. WSJ CYD MW FJXQS YM MCJ
FJXQSSQSX, WSJ CYD MW GYQM
IWZ AYMTZQMR, YSE QM PYSSWM
FJ CYDMJSJE.

9. KTRUWLHG TR WL TLIWPXWCPG
WTK RDJGUTJGR UD HPGWO ITRTDL,
WLK RVWHG TR W NOGWU PGLR.

10. OPR JDLR DM NRTSOU XTBOQ
OD NR NDWV BV OPR PRTWO DM
RLRWU APBJH.

Answers on pages 102–103.

Albert Camus

(1913–1960)

1. LPIMI BO FC ACYI CH ABHI
EBLPCTL WIORXBM CH ABHI.

2. EI ED QYIENX IR TXXC RBXH IMX
OEZU; EI ED XZRYJM IR NPSRH
QRH EI.

3. FLGWG NX J FNIG CRW ANENZM
JZO J FNIG CRW MNENZM
GVSWGXXNRZ FR ANCG.

4. LF TJKY CJY UJX CXBAWBCDFK
BAYU OXFIY YSBAOK; TFXWM BK
FAUJOS NUX YSF KTIDD UAFK.

5. WYEOS DP E VEL NH RJXXDCR
XYJ ECPVJO LJP VDXYNAX YEQDCR
EPIJB ECL WTJEO ZAJPXDNC.

6. ZC ZU DBPDHU NDUH CX WN
BXAZLDB, WRC ZC ZU DBEXUC
ZEGXUUZWBN CX WN BXAZLDB CX
CJN WZCCNY NVT.

14

7. UW DWK EVKZ KXW XMFEK ZQ BECEVD FWQZNW MPJGENEVD KXW XMFEK ZQ KXEVLEVD.

8. N DNB ZI DPOJ N DNB KUOPLAU KUJ KUZBAI UJ MJJRI KP UZDIJEH KUNB KUOPLAU KUPIJ UJ INVI.

9. RFPJ YQJMA SIQPC, EJJO TJJRFBYC MRSMHC XJMB XIQJ ADMB ADJH MQJ NIBCNFIVC IT CMHFBY.

10. QFCDC ZMVV RCACD UC JRS TKUTQMQKQC OLD QZCRQS SCJDT LO VMOC CBECDMCRNC.

Answers on pages 103–104.

Marcus Tullius Cicero

(106–43 B.C.)

1. OWS YCMOCRATCMWCRA FQGFSQOZ
GK BUR CM OG MSUQJW KGQ URY OG
KGXXGN UKOSQ OQTOW.

2. LBRMUP VBQ GNUOPH SNM, HPQXUP
VBQ RUBXLPH SNM, GNURMLP VBQ
TUPQPUJPH SNM GNU RVXQ XLQBLXRS.

3. EVZ GEV GEZ GEXH E GMTIEXH,
YOI VLVH YOI E ULLD QMDD
FLVIMVOH MV MI.

4. YVQJZNQQ MQ FJN BJVYVBFNYMQFMB
SX VYTNZF HSKFJ, VZT WYKTNZBN FJVF
SX CNRRSUNT VDN.

5. HNRGUGDMJ UX BFG FBCK GEJ
HNJRGJXG FA SUNGDJX, QDG GEJ
ZRNJBG FA RCC FGEJNX.

6. DM DIFW DYIXDK JU YQO D
UFDSS URILJVR QMSRUU OTRIR YR
D HJUR DKFJMJUOIDOJXM DO TXFR.

17

7. BJSDBEBVF VY VWEE AYYK QZYT WLBE BI VPW AZWSVWIV XYZZF YQ TSJ'I EBQW.

8. VXY ZYSTHHTHSF NK PEE VXTHSF PJY FGPEE.

9. YCIGUB HCPGS GIZ XCIIWRHZP AS CWI QCIBVOR CK IOXVZB.

10. FBY LNT JR EQZFNKY NZ FJ HNIY YIYVUJXY BNZ PQY.

Answers on pages 104–105.

René Descartes

(1596–1650)

1. SK BKGKC FBTKCHZWBT W ZXUBA HM SKOO, WBT EWQK UZ MFC MSB, WH SXKB SK XWGK TUHJMGKCKT UZ DMC MFCHKOGKH.

2. JWN XINBJNGJ TLKFG BIN RBCBUSN ZH JWN XINBJNGJ YLRNG BG ENSS BG ZH JWN XINBJNGJ YLIJDNG.

3. FBUEL YBU JTNLEF FBLTD TJLRE FBL QLEF EU RE FU XRWL FBLX GMLRD RVJ TVFLMMTNTQML, GRV RMYRPE QLEF ILDEZRJL YBRF FBLP IDUIUEL.

4. LSB TESSLA PB NBFW EAABSAGNB AL DBNBFEK AQGSMD EA AQB DECB AGCB.

5. ISDEFCPD LF LT ZJD FUCS; LZ ZUCRJDF ETV KUVLYLDF LZ.

6. GKZBDRKQ VNGVPN TRQ ONYYPN
MGK YWN RVVNRKRDUN GM YKSYW
TGKN GMYND YWRD YKSYW BYONPM.

7. AQES YTSJ YE YTSJ T OIZJ
AEWPB YOIY YOJ GJPGJG BJKJTZJ,
IPB TY TG DQWBJPY PJZJQ YE
YQWGY KESDRJYJRX YOEGJ HOE
OIZJ BJKJTZJB WG JZJP EPKJ.

8. HNBZB OG MVH VMB VS AR
SVZABZ FBDOBSG KFVWH CNOLN K
IVWFH AKR MVH FB QZVQBZDR
ZKOGBI.

9. S MN KFSEASEP, KFQZQOIZQ S
QBSDK; SEXQQX S MN M NSEX.

10. FZ FI QUZ NQUHSP ZU PEXN E
SUUO LFQO. ZPN LEFQ ZPFQS FI
ZU HIN FZ CNTT.

Answers on pages 105–106.

Benjamin Disraeli

(1804–1881)

1. NGXVK LF H STXQEZA; PHQKGGE H FVAXWWTZ; GTE HWZ H AZWAZV.

2. IADS IC DFSGUGKDSC VCTPRH RUUNZV; IADS IC TCDVS CLKCUS YCFCZDTTQ ADKKCFV.

3. FPV NVGYVF QD NWGGVNN MN GQUNFBUGT FQ LWYLQNV.

4. IUSEPDQRJRY PIQRQPRW JUS HSRSUJMMK YLS PIQRQPRW PN YLS HSRSUJYQPR YLJY QW XJRQWLQRH.

5. CBVM MW TCWLRCU LSBC MW ABRPB QC WJJWZMECRMO, MSB GWAM RGJWZMQCM MSRCU RC NRDB RA MW TCWL LSBC MW DWZUW QC QKHQCMQUB.

6. QY QT NBEG LHTQLS YD KL ESQYQEHA YGHF YD KL EDSSLEY.

7. XU RH KUBCKAUWC XOQX TUW
QMH APBUMQBX AC Q PMHQX CXHV
XU YBULGHSPH.

8. ICIEG MEYRONHBYT YP WITBOV
LOVH AI HZI MEYRONHBYT YP
ITHZOVBSVL.

9. GXA LKDA AEGABTFCA V LVB'T
RBKPZAUIA KM PXVG XVT YAAB
UKBA, GXA IDAVGAD PFZZ YA XFT
JKPAD KM RBKPFBI PXVG GK UK.

10. YVFRSH BYI HSF YQEYIX KLRHP
MYZZRHGXX; KNF FMGLG RX HS
MYZZRHGXX ERFMSNF YVFRSH.

Answers on page 106.

Albert Einstein

(1879–1955)

1. XLP RDX XD QAYDFA I FIR DB JWYYAJJ, QWX LIXEAL I FIR DB CIUWA.

2. CGXTOUNZL NQ UDOU HDNTD BCJONLQ HDCL ZLC DOQ WZBMZUUCL CACBEUDNLM DC KCOBLCG NL QTDZZK.

3. LUSZ B SCPJ SCXJF PLM LVNJMQ CQ B SCPJ HLMVNHNCSJ.

4. YNBSWLBSY NFS VODY BNYW QNZ WPS WPLFJY NFS JSWY QNZ FNWPLFJ.

5. PXHGWGU LI QSUGZGII PLBX BXG BUABX LR IVSZZ VSBBGUI QSRRHB KG BUAIBGC LR LVYHUBSRB SJJSLUI.

6. AXYAB QU HBOA UAOKWU ABL ALUA FR LPVLXQLKIL.

7. XCB WJQWRWQIGM OCN CGT BKEBHWBJABQ TNMWXIQB OWMM JNX BGTWMU DBANVB G RWAXWV NS VGTT TIFFBTXWNJ.

8. XGJHJ UW QZXGUQV RUDUQJ KOZPX TZHXKEUXS; UX UW K YPHJES GPTKQ KAAKUH.

9. FTO HCAXO NP C BCU QTNXAE JO QOOU SU DTCF TO VSHOQ CUE UNF SU DTCF TO SQ CJAO FN KOMOSHO.

10. RSJ UA MSSEUAH WAC GSTFLONOACUAH UI AWQBLO'I TSIQ DOWBQUKBM HUKQ.

Answers on page 107.

George Eliot
(Marion Evans Cross)

(1819–1880)

1. MKP JQW'I QCQI GHQ KBTQ MKP JQW'I JQJMHBQI; ZLQC GHQ IZHMWFQIZ UMH ZLBWFI G KMWF YGC MUU.

2. SDXV SK AXGG MKJOXQI QJ BUVKL VDK OXQLUYG KXCKILKJJ BU YLUKM DBOK.

3. IN PFVK YMBJ CFH JFKMNV MB IAOK QCPNV KC FV, BCK MB IAOK IN MPOTMBN PMTAK AOLN DNNB.

4. FGJ HPFGSPHX QJU FIHUC VFJXU HPQC VU QJU.

5. SPNGGNQ WG VUN ZLK YUA, ULOWKM KAVUWKM VA GLJ, LSGVLWKG RTAZ MWOWKM WK YATQG NOWQNKFN AR VUN RLFV.

6. EKNMN GW O JMNOE ZNOI RS DYCOHHNZ XRDYEMV GY DW.

7. PYLU EW PI GMFI XWS MX DWU UW OLJI UYI PWSGE GITT EMXXMAZGU XWS ILAY WUYIS?

8. FTJD J YKMET JCX ZJQT NDMTCXY; FTJD J YPLFE JCX ZJQT FDMCOETY.

9. QEC UBKL HC MQQV LQ OEQT LPC DBWBVJ QN ZRXREZ.

10. ASH GCCGJ JRLTT RHBUCT DLRY SJ MHAV BMBH, BWG DYBR DC YBUC QCCW VBPCJ SJ DYBR DC BHC.

Answers on pages 107–108.

Epictetus

(60– ?)

1. OVV WXAVYGYWXJ VANG AP LBY
BYUIG, GZGLOAP OPI OEGLOAP.

2. Y OZXA DLNZK IDK KD JW ZWFQ
JH DIW YIRZDU, IDU FXSW JH Y
OXINFW ZDAW.

3. CG JDYZJFDCQX CQ CZ MFDX
FNZX QY VCGS N VDCFGS; CG
NSMFDZCQX GYQBCGK CZ ZY
SCVVCTHOQ.

4. RH YBB EKZ YIIYRGQ LI BRIZ
BZE RE SZ CLOG UGZYE AYGZ HLE
EL KOGE CLOG TRHP LG LIIZHP
CLOG FOPUTZHE.

5. BOZGWP AHF FH HFPZOV TPGF
FPZN VPHQUE ZGF, RQF ZGF GV
RZWHXZV NHQ GAE RZ VJUZAF.

6. YT XEY KU SCNN MRT KU YTV
XEUVNC TS RKXUNQS.

7. V D B B D Y H I Z D·K M   N A̤ K   Z F D L W M
Z F N Z   M F R J   J F N Z   C K L   N A K .

8. G V Y   G E B   F B E Y N P   E V W K V
K B U P G W G O G Y   J   E W P Y   L J U   J N Y
G V B P Y   B X   A Y J N W U R   J U M
X B N A Y J N W U R .

9. V Y X Y J   G S I   T E   S V I U M L V D ,   " L
Z T G U   L U , "   K W U   G S I ,   " L   D S X Y   L U
K S H N . "

10. P M J   Q S U   D F   O U H O U Q O D W F   O A
P M J   U F H F G   F U N F G   O U   S   Q M U N F R N
C K F G F   H O Q N M G P   O R   U M N   O U   P M J G
L M C F G .

Answers on pages 108–109

Epicurus

(341–270 B.C.)

1. EHMXCI GWQNBNCN QWC BQ
IMKBQO OTHMC UWNNHNNBWQN,
VSC BQ IMKBQO PHE EMQCN.

2. NDVCARWV LA UJV CHAVZMV KX
NCLZ LZ UJV HKFT CZF KX
UWKRHDVA LZ UJV AKRD.

3. PWQ ULXQ CER PWLRVX HI IECQ
GTXP QRHTOW PH EBHLJ KQLRO
JQXNLXQJ.

4. X QXP NJB WXLKGK MGXF
WXPPBA CG MFGG MFBQ MGXF.

5. AN AB LZN BZ DXJE ZXQ
TQAVLFB' EVKC NEON EVKCB XB
OB NEV JZLTAFVLJV ZT NEVAQ
EVKC.

6. CMCYX BER FEUUCU SVQ SJ
TDJC EU QOSVAO OC OEK HVUQ
ZCCR ZSYR.

7. STRCKZ DTFQ FVEZTK QLKV
XFQZ LBRKHZN: JZ QLKV XFBXZTB
FLTKZPYZK JCVE VEZ EZRPCBI FD
FLT FJB PCYZK.

8. FMQ UWQRFQVF BWLDF ZB
VQHB-VLBBDNDQJNO DV BWQQYZI.

9. KC KM FUKS CE UMG EA CWJ
OEZM LWUC U TUS KM DUQUHNJ EA
MRQQNIKSO AEY WKTMJNA.

10. ERNOJEI YWNJYAJDY W VWE
LOR JY ERN YWNJYAJDU LJNO W
PJNNPD.

Answers on page 109.

Desiderius Erasmus

(1469–1536)

Desiderius Erasmus

1. ZMVYC OMV OVAQW EVZ BLNC
TVVB DVT ZMC XVVT DCQQVO ZV
UVBC JE ZMTVAIM ZMC WVVT OJQQ
MLSC MJB ZMTAYZ AXVE ZMCB
ZMTVAIM ZMC UCJQJEI.

2. LJNKN WP YG PNYPN WY
EGVWYH LJN CYNN TYZ YGL LJN
JNTKL.

3. OJL XNQYQXY XR PLY QV VX
MWCQXEV (WV LWHJ KQCZ JWV JQV
XBY VXYS), OJWO QO QV
QPNXVVQKUL OX VWOQVRI
LMLCIKXZI.

4. BJ JBA MAPZAKHP D HDXABH
HEDH OP KJBKADXAQ.

5. G YGXM XC NWXJHY REK FO
GYRKPHW YGXM; PGFXK XC
RJHWTRSH FO PGFXK.

6. GA ODK IBKEHO JW E HGAMVK GATGFGTYEV, ODK QEHHGJAH EBK EO ZEB ZGOD ODK BKEHJA.

7. YUQ KU KFQ EHZM YFUOQ ABVZRQ VO HEYHSO UZ EQHNQ UD HJOQZRQ.

8. CG XCZ XIW I MILEGM TZZK IW I BZOEH LIE RGYIOWG CG XIW BZOEH, JW EZX I UGWDGYNIRKG TZZK RGYIOWG CG'W HUZXE ZKM.

9. NO FVG EDAJ BIL GWBIZG NFW WVIADK, FVNW VGICF IQWD KNQQ EG IEQG FD ODCPGF JDY.

10. LT MLIJFR MXHX NCQYXJ CI ULOUQB CI RFSXB, SFGFJB MFYQJ SXXJ OFQJ.

Answers on page 110.

Mohandas Gandhi

(1869–1948)

1. SEJH GEOHVWKXOB OK DV
OWHVSOSL MG KMJNK EDEHNL SM
RH GMJVW OV SXOK ZMENW.

2. AXF NCLU ZFQANF PL YCNZWF
PL UYF ICLU ZFGAMF YF QPX
ITLQAOFM UMCUY.

3. B WBU MS SRI IMOLT IJEE
OBOREP HR YZMGXZYERTT JU ZJT
TARRDZ; ZR IJEE WRBTGOR RNROP
IMOL.

4. XUCPC QR LHPC XH JQVC XUMY
QYNPCMRQYI QXR RGCCO.

5. PLNPLPKM BKVPZPLE JNKMV
SMVNMYKPRL PB RLM'B VPEAK, JLI
PK PKB RGL VMGJVI.

6. SU LIU HIZCK OUFIJ VZ LDD
VOLV SLJ RZEDUJV LRK EUJV FR
VOU EXPZRU LPU.

7. JZ JX M BJYYJRQ ZJBWX
AWZZWE ZR MSSWME HQZEHW
AWUREW ZFW CREYT ZFMQ ZR AW
HQZEHW ZR RHEXWYIWX.

8. UBUIDSOU EV Q MQF WOHS
REJVUMP, LWH HRUIU QIU VSJU
FUMM-JQIGUT ISQTV.

9. GYY FZEGTHRX HA QTC
ZTBHWHBCB GTB HTBHWHAHKYC
NGEHYX, GTB CGIF QTC QN ZA HA
SCAJQTAHKYC NQS RFC EHABCCBA
QN GYY RFC QRFCSA.

10. DJT BRVXT WG NPZTQDS
ZTBWATX R AWBFTQS PG DJT
YQPBT DW ZT YRPL PX CJWNTXRNT
LTXDQVBDPWU WG DJWXT CJW RQT
DW TUIWS NPZTQDS.

Answers on pages 110–111.

Johann Wolfgang von Goethe

(1749–1832)

1. EMBMZWY LXMWP WBX EZMWH
TQBTMLH WYIWDP HMBX HQ
TZMWHM VQZZLGYM ALPTVLMS.

2. XRKZIJDK ZYG RFSK ZDK HLK
XMYMFYI FE NDKZH GKKGI.

3. FIH IHSHL RFHB BF ECL CB
NZHI FIH KFHBI'V AIFN NZHLH FIH
MB RFMIR.

4. SEI GIIG MY IDIKHSEMCO, SEI
ORWKH MY CWSEMCO.

5. TGO HFWJ VFGAC YFLCLYVGC
AO OWVFAOS TWCG YNGLCND VFLO
PD JFLV VFGD VFAOB NLRSFLPNG.

6. YNPO SZFSUZ INTZ PF HNKZ FX
IMZAK YFPZO IAUU IMZO HFYZ
PZNKUO IF IMZ ZPW FX AI, NPW
FIMZKD WF CJDI IMZ DNYZ VAIM
IMZAK IAYZ.

44

7. ZQ ZX DHAG CPXZCJ QY JCAYEFZBC CJJYJ QGPF QY OZFL QJHQG.

8. BUNQLBR LG IUDV NVDDLFOV NQZB LRBUDZBMV LB ZMNLUB.

9. XW DLS CVIUZ VY KNW NZ XW DLVZS VY WNDBIS, XD XZ DLS XWDSWDXVW CLXFL XZ FLXSYGM CVIDL ZDBEMXWA.

10. EQC QGDQCPE VBQGCFCOCXE HAPPGKSC EA V OVX GP EQC RTSS BAXPBGATPXCPP AR QGP ANX RCCSGXDP VXZ EQATDQEP, RAJ EQGP DGFCP QGO EQC OCVXP AR IXANGXD GXEGOVECSU EQC QCVJEP AR AEQCJP.

Answers on pages 111–112

Thomas Henry Huxley

(1825–1895)

1. TOZBCWSRJ SX NTCQJSJE WMT QZNTX RL WMT ECDT RL NSLT.

2. NSQZ, TCMVZ NMMNC RDOTV OTOJ ZHZIJNCSDR ZGVZ, SV BMTZIGZVV OROSDVN NIYNC.

3. KPR ESXW DRAFGFSR JEY CBJJRYFST, GYFDR, USA UXX KPR EKPRY QERC EJ DUSHFSA FC QFCAED.

4. MX MG XZC SFGXKERHQ NRXC KN YCT XHFXZG XK LCUMY RG ZCHCGMCG RYV XK CYV RG GFDCHGXMXMKYG.

5. BTJYJ CZ XH RYJDBJY KCZBDWJ BTDX BTJ TDZBO AHXAMQZCHX BTDB HECXCHXZ DYJ NHYBTMJZZ FJADQZJ BTJO DYJ FDSMO DYRQJS.

6. DRI QXQIS TOE, BWQ GRINP HF
OF DIQFW OF HB GOF OB BWQ
DHIFB POS, OEP OF DKNN RD
KEBRNP ERXQNBHQF DRI WHT GWR
WOF BWQ QSQF BR FQQ BWQT.

7. CKNPU N XNL CD HKNE NLE
QHSCK, NLE FDJ UNIK AJC SLCD
USM UNLEM CUK ZHKNC GKF DR
CUK QSMEDX TDO.

8. WDVBL PGKKGL NSLNS, VN VDD
AMTAE BL AES DGLC MTL, BN GLDU
PGKKGL NSLNS PDVMBYBSJ.

9. AOF EZCA YRUSRMUF TFCSUA ZV
FXSGRAJZB JC AOF RMJUJAQ AZ
ERHF QZSTCFUV XZ AOF AOJBK
QZS ZSKOA AZ XZ DOFB JA ZSKOA
AZ MF XZBF, DOFAOFT QZS ORYF
AZ XZ JA ZT BZA.

10. ITX OEAZ KV J YJSSXO LJH

AXNXO RXJAI IK OXHI EQKA, CEI

KAYM IK TKYS J RJA'H VKKI YKAZ

XAKEZT IK XAJCYX TPR IK QEI ITX

KITXO HKRXLTJI TPZTXO.

Answers on pages 112–113.

Carl Gustav Jung

(1875–1961)

1. VGBPB JX TU SJPVG UM AUTXAJUQXTBXX KJVGUQV OEJT.

2. BSTZT GAPT ZVGTW, DSTZT LW XA BLGG RABTZ; YXF BSTZT RABTZ RZTFANLXYDTW, DSTZT GAPT LW GYIULXJ.

3. J WJH ZJHHNL ITL PKO NE VKWDTRE KH EJBNP NE JH JPLKEKZKJR QTPDNHJRKLA XKLVNYL QYHKDVWTHL.

4. UGMGC OT JWQIU KGRUAE EXGYWNIHG QTCG, TC JIMG QTCG TXRURTUE, HJIU IKTWH HJRUAE ZJRYJ HJGV OT UTH WUOGCEHIUO.

5. RQ NKZCVL AZX FSQXQAL XZ CALQSNXTAL XKQ RZSVL ZAVO EO XKQ WAXQVVQPX; RQ TFFSQKQAL WX HCNX TN BCPK EO GQQVWAD.

6. LOLUS IULJQBOL ZJF YFWAV QRJQ VKWFQJFLBQS BV QRL OLUS LVVLFIL WP IULJQBOL QRWMNRQ.

7. DE H KHY DL XHIHGMO ZE MOHQDYJ H COLIZYLDGMO MDEO SDKLOME, RSOY SO DL HMLZ XZYLXDZFL ZE SDL QFRDOL RZ RSO XZKKFYDRV.

8. AKZFIJZQ ZXAZN, FW ZNQXQ UQ YAGN J ZNFOB, HQIJOHY ZNQ GSOGQXZ SW IJOV MSFGQY.

9. VYY UIFM YD VMS BXKUBP NKQDKLITSQ VMS FKAKPKHSN MIUBX JSKXL, VYY UIFM FIPVITS UBZSQ B QKFZ BXKUBP.

10. BIX XLLNZ NPGGPDWQMPLZ; MALK ISL XLDLZZISK GVS ALIQMA.

Answers on pages 113–114.

Jiddhu Krishnamurti

(1895–1986)

1. CVKS QVKEK'R PS
XSAKERQPSALSF HY QVK RKWY,
QVKS NSHCWKAFK VPR LQR
ELFVQYXW TWPBK.

2. SXHSC RE F ESXFOAJ SCROA;
SCJ ZWXJ GWH THXEHJ RS, SCJ
ZWXJ RS KRVV JVHMJ GWH.

3. SF BSKWMFSFT UESMWBN WP
WGM WAPEHBMK PJ DFPWGMA, PEA
PZF HEAVMFK DAM KPCMWSCMK
BSTGWMFMV.

4. EWYI BQ VZ ILJGVWGPBZVGM
JABZS; UBJAWXJ BJ, EBDI BQ
HVGGIZ.

5. SWDT WQ SWCT Y PYQR GWPTG
VWRF Y AGTYR PJSNOT JD VYRTG
VWRFJNR Y XTAWBBWBA JG YB
TBKWBA.

6. JZAMURA YHVVZUD XUR NHDDUA
VBB AMB CSBBTB HOUDL AMB
PBHEBV US AMB VRDPZLMA UD AMB
JHABS.

7. NQUB-MPJKUQXRQ GN ILQ
OQRGPPGPR JB KGNXJF GP KLJNQ
ICHPDYGUUGIV HPX NGUQPAQ
ILQCQ GN ILQ GFFQHNYCHOUQ.

8. HIV OBJN HIWH BA OWNV GIEPV
LS HIEQUIH, LS MJEGPVNUV, LS
VTDVCBVJFV, BA AHBPP HIV
CVAQPH EK HBOV WJN AECCEG.

9. UH-HRMJCKBHV BO RHOOBAPM
HVPF YEMV KEMJM BO DJMMGHW
DJHW MVSF, CUTIBOBKBSMVMOO,
CVG DJHW KEM UJCSBVX DHJ
RMJOHVCP HJ UHPPMUKBSM
GHWBVCVUM, RHYMJ.

10. MXY BSM DSFU BSPM
CXEEUEEAXPE SPR EAV AP VDU
EUSV XL CXZUG, HYV ZAVDXYV
HUSYVM SPR KGUSVPUEE XL IXFU,
IALU EXXP HUNXBUE BAEUGM SPR
NXPLYEAXP.

Answers on page 114.

James Russell Lowell

(1819–1891)

1. VKC AGVTK VM CNWCTLCKDC LU YVTAG E YGVFC YLFQCTKCUU VM YETKLKO.

2. JWP ATTODMW KQU JWP UPKU KOTQP QPHPS IWKQFP JWPDS TGDQDTQM.

3. QVD FQPGA PH KXA PXD ZKX'F GDKN DUBDGTDXMD HTXIF TQF FQKGQNTXL BKGKNNDN TX QVKQ PH DYDGA PXD PH CF.

4. FBQNGXJL NF SF TLLJYXQ GB GUL NHSPNTSGNBT SF FBKNLGW NF VUBQLFBHL YBI GUL KUSISKGLI.

5. RYV EP NY DS MDDB XGYYJ JYAYANYJTKM VGCV VGY ATPSDJVEKYP GCJBYPV VD NYCJ CJY VGDPY OGTXG KYIYJ XDAY.

6. NO HIL QEGUL XM HIL
FLQHNONLQ, KDGYO YNUU OLALD
YLNJI QX BVEI GQ KDGNO.

7. LEXEWMBXT UFT PB FKNMBHBZ
ML F LFWWEJ DANBWB, PRX YFUB
ZBUFLZD YEW MXD BHMZBLKB F
UEWB ZMDXFLX FLZ AWEIELOBZ
WBHBWPBWFXMEL.

8. SJRKFV MXHMOV VQQI PMRWQW
HJQK HQ XUUL TMEL UK SJQI, MKG
RS RV UNS UP SJMS
RKMEEQVVRTXQ SUHQW UP SJQ
BMVS SJMS XUKFRKF XQMKV MKG
TQELUKV.

9. PLI FIHJW WUHIX ZUPLJZQ
EIPPIY PLOZ PLI JZPUWIYOZSI UC
YICUYGIYX, OZF FYIOFX ZUPLJZQ
XU GVSL OX PLIJY SLOYJPN OZF
BOPJIZSI.

10. QRP VCFH YELQR QREQ SPETN
SPFF ECK RVFKN LQN JVFVT LC
EFF SPEQRPTN LN QREQ SRLJR LN
SVAPC VY JVCALJQLVC ECK NPQ
SLQR QRP NRETW ZVTKECQ VY
PGWPTLPCJP.

Answers on page 115.

Maimonides
(Moses Ben Maimon)
(1135–1204)

1. UFLTL UETZR DTL ODCB DCZ JFLKT OLDCKCH KR RODWW—JFDJ KR NEWWB.

2. WOY MKXWDNDF IKBY KF WOY TNZYXUWY IKBY.

3. E YEU QMJ VZ GEFDEVU JH MVZ JQU ZJWN VZ E KOPEDPO MPOJ DMEU DMP GJYYEULPO JH MJZDZ.

4. CDV CG IAIYO VKCDMUJL LIUVKM, CJI BM LDI VC VKI HYDIPVO CG JUVDYI; UPP VKI CVKIYM UYI HUDMIL QO VKI MVDZBLBVO CG XUJ.

5. PJ GPB YBDTM EHDRIYJTK DX TJIHXDXC GDTT FJUBQJ GDMJ.

6. P YPEE AIBOCQT VT IHIVPIB JT NQHGICOPHR OFIV OQ SCPIHAB.

7. WR URQ SC ZTHOVHT RT LRTH
ZARTSRXC VPOW VPH URQ RG
ZAOMMHWSWZ VPH PHOTVC RG VPH
DRRT, VPH JSMRJC, VPH RTDPOWC
OWM VPH CVTOWZHTC.

8. MLZVNVY TDPVI NZMI EO ZYWVY
SZ WEIQEGCEOV LEI TZYDC
WEIGZIESEZO DOW SZ ETGYZNV
LEI QZOWRQS, WEIGCDKI
QZTTVOWDHCV JVDC DOW EI
MZYSLK ZX GYDEIV.

9. GEUBJBQ INPRFZCP HBQMC YU
UYEBQP GNFF KB OQZXYBI HBQMC
ENHPBFT.

10. QP F OFY MZMSGQIMI RTBMS,
JQI LSQMPI FYC BTSSQMI BQAA
FGGHOHAFXM.

Answers on page 116.

John Stuart Mill

(1806–1873)

1. OI EOP RPIQ LZBCONZF VIYLGQI NC NQ COI YGQCPW WLDIQ ZP YOPNYI.

2. MOD FLRNOIQT JCIKCIN FLR MNI CMBBF, MEZ FLR GIMOI KL UI OL.

3. NCC PTTJ KYDEPM BYDAY HZDMK NUH KYH WUVDKM TW TUDPDENCDKX.

4. OLOAPHBO TKH AOYOZLOE JKO WAHJOYJZHB HQ NHYZOJP HTON U AOJSAB QHA JKO MOBOQZJ.

5. FKDS HKI HLZBQ LDK LAYK BJ BKYY BOKVD JIU QBJDS IVBOJGB ZJEEKUBQ BJ ADVUW JGB BOKVD EKLUVUW.

6. GXUKTCTS NSEMXTM VYJVCVJEUDVKB VM JTMOQKVMA, HB GXUKTCTS YUAT VK AUB HT NUDDTJ.

7. BFF DPBD RBCKX KNZXDKVQK
WBFIBUFK DG BVHGVK EKSKVEX GV
DPK KVMGYQKRKVD GM
YKXDYBZVDX ISGV DPK BQDZGVX
GM GDPKY SKGSFK.

8. PLC NCBPUQ UBA NRFUQ, QOJC
PLC NGVIGQUF ZRMCFV, UFC
ONZFRHCA RBQD YD YCOBW GVCA.

9. RVYPAO EZY FYGC NMVZWXV
JMVVGC PY ZY ZWKFOLXVMV FJ
JMVVQFK.

10. BO SJ SJLJ HJKJL FY UDF YH
YGL YRBHBYHZ, QJDUGZJ FPYZJ
YRBHBYHZ CUX QJ SLYHT, SJ
ZPYGWI WJUKJ UWW YGL
BHFJLJZFZ GHDULJI OYL, UHI UWW
YGL IGFBJZ GHRJLOYLCJI.

Answers on pages 116–117.

Jean Baptiste Molière
(1622–1673)

1. ZAHY JRXH'V LENA MOYV VDRRNAJC QN DEGHV JQKH EV TOJJ EV FEY SH.

2. JAQ KXBIW FBSRP ARU R AQRXJ NYJ NBX R MIQQP; JAQ GIPPYPZ FBSRP YU GQOQTXRJQW NBX AQX FYJ, RPW JAQ NBBO NBX AQX EYPW PRJIXQ.

3. DRP DNJP UPMDBPYGM EW RP TRK MPLPN IKGWDW GIKJD GMCDREMU.

4. JKLVAJM AT PCTAPB ZVPJ KJP AT BAFV LVCJ LK IP CJ VKJPTL WCJ; AL'T ZVPJ KJP AT OKKB LVCL AL IPFKWPT YAEEAFHNL.

5. SJX DAXESXMS KXETFXMM PO CXF NM SJXNA MSAPFD ESSEBJCXFS SP WNOX.

6. HGIFI OU SL FIECFK UL KIAODGHWYA, SL BAICUYFI UL IZVYOUOHI, CU GCTOSD LSI'U ELFJ JSLES CSK CNNACOPIK QX HGLUI EGLUI CBBACYUI NLSWIFU GLSLF.

7. JB ZJI JYU KBGBX PBBK XLRLECAICU LU CKYPAB OI AYCQJ.

8. QZGAV WZFU-LBKCFZIPZ, CVYAV YW QVZ VZYPVQ KU GFF CYWIKO, GBI LBKCFZIPZ QK KQVZDW, CVYAV YW QVZ OGDL KU QDSZ SBIZDWQGBIYBP.

9. PKN VLNFPNL PKN TGIPFZON, PKN QTLN VOTLD BX TUNLZTQBXV BP.

10. BC BP ASC SAEI JOUC JN QS, RXC UEPS JOUC JN QS ASC' QS, GSH JOBDO JN UHN· UDDSXACUREN.

Answers on pages 117–118.

George Edward Moore

(1873–1958)

1. OCEWLK RQKU NORKKR UKE BNJNEU EQ XDCE NU IQUUNMBK.

2. GJ KOG JM GIL VLYSWGY JH VLHWLOGEJM EY IKVXWA LBLV TEYL.

3. BAXRJITX FJ CXTO CRAIRSAX RJ R NXRQJ PU WXXB IJ HFP HUT VUFQK UPZXT PZFQKJ.

4. BYCGC SX DEZDLX D GSOYB DAU D ZGFAO ZDL, DAU BYC ZGFAO ZDL DEZDLX XCCHX BYC HFGC GCDXFADVEC.

5. GIZ ABM MDZ FLTATFD SYZGFVIZF HBIZ TAMZAFZ?

6. MCPUWR UW LQEPLDXMEVO WLSMYUPY XP ZVXYLUWR ZW Z EPIXYUQM PN RMZQW.

7. QRP'X HJYV, SR MRV
AMDYSGJZMD XSYJMYSQR, SX YQ
HQ YKMY MGYSQR TKSGK TSZZ
GMJXP LQDP NQQH YKMR MRV
AQXXSCZP MZYPDRMYSUP.

8. MQROFV WEVQ ZMFOZM TL YRXQ
OV WMXLQ SC NTTZ.

9. BM JLCOC GC SAW MOCC XBEE,
JLCA BJ BZ VGYBVDZEW VAC VM
JLC NSDZCZ XC LSYC JV OCNUVA
XBJL, BA NVAZBPCOBAF LVX QDNL
FVVP BZ TVZZBGEC.

10. CLRZAI ZA VOC WRXVJZKC
MOZXO ORSWA VONV MC RYLOV
CNXO RD YA VR GYJAYC RYJ RMK
LJCNVCAV ONGGZKCAA NA RYJ
YSVZINVC CKW.

Answers on pages 118–119.

Ayn Rand

(1905–1982)

1. ST ECMYC GE RY ST ZETGCEF
EB UEVC FSBY, UEV JPXY GE JPXY
P WVCWEAY—P WCEMVZGSXY
WVCWEAY.

2. HEOQ NOQ AEKDO SEO AKNO
TKABY GDONBAO, BS BA SEO NXAS
YXQABASOQS XQOA HEX HBQ.

3. PXM WZIFLMIIARL'I PTTE FI
NREZMI; PXM WZQMRZHQRP'I PTTE
FI OMRQ.

4. ZOQ JGSA IC GD OIDQTZ JGD FT
ZOGZ OQ JQGDT XOGZ OQ TGWT
GDM ADIXT XOGZ OQ JQGDT.

5. YXTJXTS CRW HORY JXT GXUNT
RP U NTIIFT RS JXT GJSWDJWST RP
U GRFUS GCGJTL, JXT UMERLG
STLUEO JXT GULT: JXUJ EJ
TMEGJG UOK JXUJ CRW HORY EJ.

6. RMG'X QLXUGX FPG JLHLZGW
RMJO CO ZUG DRQGP RB RMG'X
AFMA.

7. YW SYH NW Y CGNHJ TR WGUR-
SYIG EGYUZF, WT NW FG Y CGNHJ
TR WGUR-SYIG WTAU.

8. BDGJ UDG RMXGQU PGJ UITJ
EJUV FVBRTLQ, UDG RNGTRHG PGJ
UITJ EJUV MTIUGQ.

9. P GZBPAKQW QIPQ IZALN MRRL
PN P SAPKG, IZALN RGJQKMRNN—
MZM-RYKNQRMSR—PN KQN
NQPMLPBL ZE TPAFR.

10. R UGLYB NRZ BLQW ZLV
ZQJRVQ EXW LOZ XBQZVXVT.

Answers on pages 119–120.

George Santayana

(1863–1952)

1. OXX OQCSUSIVL QJLU CR
WRTROURW PKRV UKRB OLF TID
UKR SQNILLSCXR.

2. VGYJ Y AJSYZDN RQNYALSN
JGNSN XA AWKNJXKNA XZ ANNXZD
VGYJ VN NURNIJ, WS GNYSXZD
VGYJ VN PZNV VYA HYIJ!

3. UKF UKT AVHJ ZP EP KAPFJ SPY
K NKAH, IRZ GJ GKZJC ZP CZKFB
KAPFJ VF GVC PDVFVPFC.

4. PKO TCNDR ZHD IKC KHX DCP
IOLP EX H XHUHRO, HDW PKO CYW
ZHD IKC IEYY DCP YHNRK EX H
GCCY

5. WDWCP MNFFEYX, GESW GELW
NF N RBYGW, BNF EOF LWWO EX
YXW UYCNG JGEUNOW NXA EOF
BWNA EX NXYOBWC.

6. JDUZFJV KZD QGHB KUCD
PEWGEKB QT XFG EV ZEV
YFJFYEKB KQ PDVJEVD ZEXVDHT.

7. KAN ANBXK ABQ XNBQTPQ TI
UAHFA KAN XNBQTP ABQ PT
VPTUWNGZN.

8. ZXWUNUBW ZX WEU IESXPZXP
BUSBMXB ZB S VCIE ESJJZUN
BWSWU MY VZXQ WESX FUZXP
EMJURUBBRH ZX RMKU GZWE
BJNZXP.

9. WGU EVURW NMIIMHZKWS MY
UNZHRWMPY MO WP EUW
UDCUVMUYHU PZW PI MNURO.

10. E CBRR OLYN NGRW YGI
OREWHBR IZR DGBIZ GC EYMIZLYP
TM IZR DGBIZ GC EYMIZLYP RUWR.

Answers on pages 120–121.

Albert Schweitzer

(1875–1965)

1. JQ JF QTV MDQV BM VCVIP QILQT QB EV DU BEOVKQ BM IJXJKLYV NTVU JQ JF MJIFQ DKKYDJHVX.

2. YJV ZYOEFAVO YJV OVPVOVFUV MEO FIYQOIG GLMV, YJV ZYOEFAVO AOESZ IGZE YJIY MEO ZTLOLYQIG GLMV.

3. MWIPI GA GO YA KO GOAMGOHMGRI KXI GO MWI SPIAIOHI LB UGBI, BLP XI LYPAIURIA KPI ASKPEA LB MWI XGUU ML UGRI.

4. AIH JHWH THAAYCF VR EB NYTAT EB PYWAVHT MCS PYZHT YT NYLH PMJRYCF EC AIH LHUDEMWS MCS ZMNNYCF AIH HCTVYCF CEYTH JVTYZ.

5. EYQKGKV LA ACUVKJ CKVAQXUM
CULX SRAW IKKM YLSAKMI BUMMKJ
WQ YKMC LX JLSLXLAYLXH WYK
CULX QI QWYKVA.

6. LES EXFESWL VJHKCSMFS XW LH
VJHK LEGL KS GTS WDTTHDJMSM
UZ IZWLSTZ.

7. OW RPO QX FDFT IWRCKFJFKU
POY CFTRPOFOJKU P XJTPOSFT JW
VQX NFKKWH RPO. RPO AFKWOSX
JW RPO.

8. IRQC TE VUC CVCBPMI VUTPY
OUTWU SCP WMP MIBCMZK RP
CMBVU JREECEE ME TV BCMIIK TE.

9. BQ RMQ RVBRAG BRVIJFX PF
VPPGQ GLPFQG BYJEY PDQMYRFX
LYQ SMQEJSJEQ PC SQGGJNJGN.

10. ECG XFECQFV BWZH NHXGWBGPE EZ XGWBGPE WGPZJYNLGK EWOEC RGFKA ECWZOJC ECG SFRRGV ZB WGFRNEV.

Answers on page 121.

Lucius Annaeus Seneca

(4 B.C.–65 A.D)

1. ZP INN PONVDVWVOX, WLO
SZXW DLIHSVTF VX WLIW ZP I PVHS
ITB FOTWNO PHVOTBXLVU.

2. KL KW V AXBAUWLBXUYW
HBVQZBWW LU PUCB V NVZ
MBTUXB HB QZUH SKN, VZO ZUL
LU EVXB TUX SKN VTLBX.

3. KP KN ZYP PCM VJZ ECY CJN
PYY TKPPTM, FQP PCM VJZ ECY
OLJHMN VYLM, PCJP KN WYYL.

4. ZPQ NMF SBJJ SGB NGMKMNSBK
PX BRBKZ EMF TGBF ZPQ HBB GPT
GB KBNBARBH UKMAHB.

5. BS PN TJNF KJOSMIGH OBJ BYN
KJOSM JWSM BPTNSHI.

6. DUDQ PZWW MNX QDD PJDM XJD
JDTVX PZQJDQ XJDY XN HD
HWZMS.

7. D Y U Z T D W   T P   P Y   J R L U M T D   M P
U Z M U   U Z R   R N T K P   Y B   T F K R D R P P
J M D   E R   P Z M A R D   Y B B   E V   Z M L F
H Y L A .

8. B C   L B K   U C D C Y W C E   Z   F C A C S Y Q
L Y Q B   J U Z Q Y Q G V C   U C T Z M E   Q B C
S Y U E Q   Y A E Q Z X X I C A Q   K A   B Y E
V C F Q .

9. K L   K V   S   G Z F T J   G Z S X   L J S L
D U S X V   L Z   L J U   J U K T J L V   Z Q
T G U S L O U V V .

10. J K W C W   F A   P S J K F P O   F P   J K F A
M S C E H ,   Y W C K G Y A ,   J K G J   F A
J G E T W H   L S C W   S U ,   G P H   E W A A
X P H W C A J S S H ,   J K G P   J K W   I X A F P W A A
S U   G   K G Y Y Z   E F U W .

Answers on page 122.

George Bernard Shaw

(1856–1950)

1. AW'B VFBW NB FJRHYNBNJW WT LYW ZTOY WPNJ QTF CNOLNAJ ITO NB WT LYW HYBB.

2. CL B HGMIZO CI B JZMO LZZX, KNG LZXXS TCXX QGK TZMIG, OZK JGKKGM, JS B XZOQ XCLG'I HMBFKCFG.

3. RMH RHXR QI P JPE QD FQJPE'X UDHHGVEW VX MQF RMHC UHMPAH VE P TYPDDHZ.

4. CZUAU QAU WI RUGAUCR JUCCUA SUOC CZQW CZU RUGAUCR CZQC UXUAMJILM FHURRUR.

5. GTK XFSK GTJBOE C XCB JE CETCXKY FW, GTK XFSK SKEHKZGCDNK TK JE.

6. ZTUSLHS TZ WKS VDZW MSQASHW SEMQSZZTDL DA ZHDQL.

7. WKY OLWRTO'J QTZLPJ LZY
PRMY RWJ WYYWK: WKY QTZY
EYBLFYE WKYF LZY WKY QTZY RW
KVZWJ WT WTVBK WKYQ.

8. JWIRN VRJVMR ISDR WJJ ASBU
HSNRF JE WIRON JZB WJ WIOBC
AXHI SGJXW UJXNF.

9. DPG KAZJAGCC ZR DPG LZAFQ
QGKGXQC ZX DPG KGZKFG LPZ
AGROCG DZ SNNGKD RSNDC SXQ
EXCECD ZX DPG CSDECRSNDEZX ZR
DPGEA EXCDEXNDC.

10. LVWLK FX LKU YJU LKFJH
JYEYTG QFII EUIFUCU.

Answers on pages 122–123

Voltaire
(François-Marie Arouet)
(1694–1778)

1. ODH DFJM VS YQ XVOLOW FPL
MVPDQHOW QFW: MVK OTHHOD TH
TQ HMFH T UDFOOW RPVK!

2. ABI STMUMZ SJ IOMW BDN
DWYDHN VIIZ DZ DVHNN, ABI
EIFAB SJ YBMLB ZS SZI BDN VIIZ
DVWI AS NSQZE.

3. FGI NWVLWIJJ VE WASIWJ FV
FGI JID AJ BVF DJ WDNAY DJ FGDF
VE ODB FV IWWVW.

4. OGU DA UPW YPSU VDTLCF: MC
YCTPOCA AP, GA MC YCTPOCA
ADTL.

5. EJB VJA IOOB MKXOB
OXOPNDVKBM BOOFOF DH QKXO KB
AHGKODN; WYAD JA VO VJA IOOB
MKXOB J ADHEJGV DH FKMOAD,
ONOA DH AOO, J AHYQ DH WYFMO.

6. IMH IABH FMVAIHA WX OGJHAIZ GU GCEHDHCEHCFH, QVGCIVGCHE JZ XWAFH.

7. WK WA TRU EFKKFU KI EF AWGFJK KLRJ VFUFGN KI WJHUFRAF KLF BORJKWKN IT ERQ EIICA.

8. ULTV KDJDLPZXTJ ZT KDJDLPZXTJ IQDMZXSXIV XJSLDPIDI PJW MLTGPGXBXZC WXVXJXINDI; PJW ITTJ MLTGPGXBXZC XI LDWASDW ZT RDLT.

9. AXWIVBH XD SFAH UFT NUF WI SFAH BJI MSKIV BS TS KJUB SFI KXAAD.

10. XVT ZVT NVEU KTMH V ZUCFVBT TGXLUC KW FUUFN, NVBC VTP BPUVO.

Answers on pages 123–124.

Alfred North Whitehead

(1861–1947)

1. ZVP RSGGVW JVFWJVGI ZVPL BHGC'F QHDI PGWHQ ZVP TSEI FTSLJIGIC HW.

2. FPCHIYVEY VCYM PCX FYYB SPW GYXXYL XNSP ZDMN.

3. PME KPS ROXK RSAWXPSX WX PME KPS DCKCAS JSFMLSX.

4. HIC HDMC EQKKQUMOHR QY HG MBECDYHNBE IGF NBRHIQBT YMDLQLCY HIC ONAYC GK HQJC.

5. XTGTCE FOT OVLX'S GBBX WXTPWBC CTFX OVL SOB LQRNOSBLS XTSRTX TI FOVS SOB YBVQ RL.

6. IPB AGV'W AGWAS G UPUDVW NI WSD KAYBTT PT WSD VDAM — XW'K JPVD, IPB MVPQ.

7. OUMY UQ ADY YBIZJEYBA ZM YEZAUZB, GYTUFYG MTZE ADY HCQA CBG CUEYG CA ADY MKAKTY.

8. C SJFWJKH VY VP VWY RVPHYW RFTMHK EHRTKH VW EHIVPY WT CPCFZUH VWYHFR.

9. NOQ OGTVC RBMP EZ VC ECZNAGTQCN SBA NOQ KABMGJNEBC BS VAN EC NOQ DESQ BS NOQ OGTVC ZBGD.

10. EUMQM GI OW QWNHC QWHS EW CMHQOGOX EUQWRXU HO HGQN YHEU WK ZQGCCGHOE XMOMQHCGAHEGWOI.

Answers on pages 124–125.

Walt Whitman

(1819–1892)

1. HLRZQBZ UYTD WCO DEQB
JTYWQTBF TU WCO CQFWTYV TU
WCO PTYIR FT UEY, HLFWQNO QF
EIPEVF QB HOTJEYRV.

2. NDD MNCDPX YNK RF MZSULJFQ
ZM ALY HAZ ANX GFSMFIP INQEZS.

3. NREQ ZPLAPJE EM VMZUW
KRZEIP MZ EM QPZMRLV UOG
ZPWRBRMIL ROJIVYPOJT, EQP MWG
AZROJRAWPL ZPVURO.

4. LAR MT ARYRX RANMXREW
UMNZLFN NZR MATNMAIN LD
ELLPMAQ KXLFAJ.

5. JHY HLHUB OVP JDDR YD
GNOWHJT. YGHP WDINHYB FNJJ
YVRH IVUH DT NYWHJT.

6. LPP BOLB L CKYNSU TSKN SY
BODUGN DN SH ZSUNKAMKUZK.

7. RGX HGXZWF CB T CBJJBE
LZFDB XY T STP'H JTWBPJH JGTP
JGB STP GOSHBWY?

8. V ZSS QW LSXZWQ PJE PS
ZJWGHY HSO WGL HVCJOZ ZJVQS
GQYSL IGZJSHZ.

9. FJDM ZN JVBDXZMW ZX ZMN
QDZMJ, YUGR, JRHUZNB, SURMHW,
RGRX BUHDYN, CVM RBUMZUX?

10. QU QETVR UA CKK QEPDP
BUVMPND UA STQO CVM SUJVQNO,
CVM BP QCRP VU TVQPNPDQ TV
QEPW.

Answers on pages 125–126.

Oscar Wilde

(1854–1900)

1. YQP ABFJ YQKBL YQXY ABP
VPXFFJ MBACG XEAZY QZNXB
BXYZVP KG YQXY KY RQXBLPG.

2. G JGO SNW XWYQ OWV VNMOT
RWD NMJQYUR, XWYQ OWV VNMOT
GV GUU.

3. RI SLW JWQQE JOW JHMJO, SLW
RE EMHW, ESSLWH SH QVJWH, JS
NW ISMLF SMJ.

4. HM UMKI MBIEIUA LE HXI
GIDLBBLBD MA C ULAI-UMBD
YMJCBVI.

5. NIHN AJYBNZF QX NIM ZQAIMXN
CIQAI BJYZQXIMX NIM DZMHNMXN
BYLVMZ JG BJVUM HBT IHOOF
IYLHB VMQBDX.

6. RABFB WN QK NWQ BCTBSR
NROSWJWRG.

7. J YRDLY LQ J XJD KMH SDHKQ
FMP VTLYP HW PGPTRFMLDA JDU
FMP GJEZP HW DHFMLDA. .

8. JIYAF NKA QTAX XI HK
WTLXPWYS, TAE TVK AIX; ISE NKA
QTAX XI HK WTLXPSKZZ, TAE
RTAAIX.

9. OQUEUFUH J IJE KTUW J
DQTHTLNQAZ WDLBYK DQYEN, YD
YW JAOJZW XHTI DQU ETRAUWD
ITDYFUW.

10. YW LHW LPP MI FGW DCFFWH,
QCF XAZW AJ CX LHW PAANMID LF
FGW XFLHX.

Answers on page 126.

Answers

St. Thomas Aquinas

1. Charity brings to life again those who are spiritually dead.

2. Justice is a certain rectitude of mind whereby a man does what he ought to do in the circumstances confronting him.

3. Every mind grasps those things that are most common, such as being, one, and good.

4. Law is an ordinance of reason for the common good, made by him who has care of the community.

5. All men alike, both guilty and innocent, die the death of nature.

6. The life of grace has the nature, not of an end, but of something that is a means toward an end.

7. There is no kind of sin which is not sometimes due to the demons' suggestion.

8. The human soul understands itself through its own act of understanding, showing perfectly its power and nature.

9. Man can of his own accord fall into sin, but he cannot advance towards merit without divine assistance.

10. Reason in man is rather like God in the world.

Pearl Buck

1. We human beings are the only creatures who are able to think of our own end, without doubt or faith.

2. If a man comes to do his own good for you, then must you flee that man and save yourself.

3. When the people of any country choose peace at all costs, not even generals can make war.

4. It is better to learn early of the inevitable depths, for then sorrow and death take their proper place in life, and one is not afraid.

5. Without love, it is easy to believe that death is final, but with it—impossible!

6. No man knows what an American will construct when he is able to afford his own house.

7. Time and the stream pass on.

8. One has to begin at the beginning, one has to wait for maturity, and it cannot be hastened.

9. Distance is an invaluable aid sometimes to clear vision, and space is a great lens.

10. The love of beauty waits to be born in the heart of every child.

Albert Camus

1. There is no love of life without despair of life.

2. It is futile to weep over the mind; it is enough to labor for it.

3. There is a time for living and a time for giving expression to life.

4. We must put our principles into great things; mercy is enough for the small ones.

5. Charm is a way of getting the answer yes without having asked any clear question.

6. It is always easy to be logical, but it is almost impossible to be logical to the bitter end.

7. We get into the habit of living before acquiring the habit of thinking.

8. A man is more a man through the things he keeps to himself than through those he says.

9. Like great works, deep feelings always mean more than they are conscious of saying.

10. There will never be any substitute for twenty years of life experience.

Marcus Tullius Cicero _____

1. The distinguishing property of man is to search for and to follow after truth.

2. Nature has formed you, desire has trained you, fortune has preserved you for this insanity.

3. Any man may make a mistake, but none but a fool will continue in it.

4. Rashness is the characteristic of ardent youth, and prudence that of mellowed age.

5. Gratitude is not only the greatest of virtues, but the parent of all others.

6. An army abroad is but a small service unless there be a wise administration at home.

7. Inability to tell good from evil is the greatest worry of man's life.

8. The beginnings of all things are small.

9. Morals today are corrupted by our worship of riches.

10. The aim of justice is to give everyone his due.

René Descartes

1. We never understand a thing so well, and make it our own, as when we have discovered it for ourselves.

2. The greatest minds are capable of the greatest vices as well as of the greatest virtues.

3. Those who digest their ideas the best so as to make them clear and intelligible, can always best persuade what they propose.

4. One cannot be very attentive to several things at the same time.

5. Pleasure is in the soul; it touches and modifies it.

6. Ordinary people may settle for the appearance of truth more often than truth itself.

7. From time to time I have found that the senses deceive, and it is prudent never to trust completely those who have deceived us even once.

8. There is not one of my former beliefs about which a doubt may not be properly raised.

9. I am thinking, therefore I exist; indeed I am a mind.

10. It is not enough to have a good mind. The main thing is to use it well.

Benjamin Disraeli

1. Youth is a blunder; manhood a struggle; old age a regret.

2. What we anticipate seldom occurs; what we least expect generally happens.

3. The secret of success is constancy to purpose.

4. Predominant opinions are generally the opinions of the generation that is vanishing.

5. Next to knowing when to seize an opportunity, the most important thing in life is to know when to forgo an advantage.

6. It is much easier to be critical than to be correct.

7. To be conscious that you are ignorant is a great step to knowledge.

8. Every production of genius must be the production of enthusiasm.

9. The more extensive a man's knowledge of what has been done, the greater will be his power of knowing what to do.

10. Action may not always bring happiness; but there is no happiness without action.

Albert Einstein

1. Try not to become a man of success, but rather a man of value.

2. Education is that which remains when one has forgotten everything he learned in school.

3. Only a life lived for others is a life worthwhile.

4. Sometimes one pays most for the things one gets for nothing.

5. Whoever is careless with the truth in small matters cannot be trusted in important affairs.

6. Truth is what stands the test of experience.

7. The individual who has experienced solitude will not easily become a victim of mass suggestion.

8. There is nothing divine about mortality; it is a purely human affair.

9. The value of a man should be seen in what he gives and not in what he is able to receive.

10. Joy in looking and comprehending is nature's most beautiful gift.

George Eliot (Marion Evans Cross)

1. Old men's eyes are like old men's memories; they are strongest for things a long way off.

2. What we call despair is often the painful eagerness of unfed hope.

3. We must find our duties in what comes to us, not in what we imagine might have been.

4. Our thoughts are often worse than we are.

5. Blessed is the man who, having nothing to say, abstains from giving in words evidence of the fact.

6. There is a great deal of unmapped country in us.

7. What do we live for if not to make the world less difficult for each other?

8. Wear a smile and have friends; wear a scowl and have wrinkles.

9. One must be poor to know the luxury of giving.

10. Our deeds still travel with us from afar, and what we have been makes us what we are.

Epictetus

1. All philosophy lies in two words, sustain and abstain.

2. A ship ought not to be held by one anchor, nor life by a single hope.

3. In prosperity it is very easy to find a friend; in adversity nothing is so difficult.

4. In all the affairs of life let it be your great care not to hurt your mind or offend your judgment.

5. Preach not to others what they should eat, but eat as becomes you and be silent.

6. No man is free who is not master of himself.

7. Difficulties are things that show what men are.

8. The two powers which constitute a wise man are those of bearing and forbearing.

9. Never say of anything, "I lost it," but say, "I gave it back."

10. You can be invincible if you never enter in a contest where victory is not in your power.

Epicurus

1. Wealth consists not in having great possessions, but in having few wants.

2. Pleasure is the absence of pain in the body and of troubles in the soul.

3. The wise man thinks of fame just enough to avoid being despised.

4. A man who causes fear cannot be free from fear.

5. It is not so much our friends' help that helps us as the confidence of their help.

6. Every man passes out of life as though he had just been born.

7. Praise from others must come unasked: we must concern ourselves with the healing of our own lives.

8. The greatest fruit of self-sufficiency is freedom.

9. It is vain to ask of the gods what a man is capable of supplying for himself.

10. Nothing satisfies a man who is not satisfied with a little.

Desiderius Erasmus _____

1. Those who would not make room for the poor fellow to come in through the door will have him thrust upon them through the ceiling.

2. There is no sense in bowing the knee and not the heart.

3. The opinion of men is so various (as each bird has his own song), that it is impossible to satisfy everybody.

4. No one respects a talent that is concealed.

5. A nail is driven out by another nail; habit is overcome by habit.

6. In the breast of a single individual, the passions are at war with the reason.

7. Woe to the land whose prince is always on leave of absence.

8. He who was a damned fool as a young man because he was young, is now a respectable fool because he's grown old.

9. If the body can escape its shadow, this heart also will be able to forget you.

10. If wisdom were valued as highly as money, nobody would need gold

Mohandas Gandhi _____

1. True friendship is an identity of souls rarely to be found in this world.

2. One must become as humble as the dust before he can discover truth.

3. A man of few words will rarely be thoughtless in his speech; he will measure every word.

4. There is more to life than increasing its speed.

5. Infinite striving after perfection is one's right, and it its own reward.

6. We are proud heirs to all that was noblest and best in the bygone age.

7. It is a million times better to appear untrue before the world than to be untrue to ourselves.

8. Everyone is a law unto himself, but there are some well-marked roads.

9. All humanity is one undivided and indivisible family, and each one of us is responsible for the misdeeds of all the others.

10. The cause of liberty becomes a mockery if the price to be paid is wholesale destruction of those who are to enjoy liberty.

Johann Wolfgang von Goethe ————————

1. General ideas and great conceit always tend to create horrible mischief.

2. Pleasure and love are the pinions of great deeds.

3. One never goes so far as when one doesn't know where one is going.

4. The deed is everything, the glory is nothing.

5. Men show their character in nothing more clearly than by what they think laughable.

6. Many people take no care of their money till they come nearly to the end of it, and others do just the same with their time.

7. It is much easier to recognize error than to find truth.

8. Nothing is more terrible than ignorance in action.

9. In the works of man as in those of nature, it is the intention which is chiefly worth studying.

10. The highest achievement possible to a man is the full consciousness of his own feelings and thoughts, for this gives him the means of knowing intimately the hearts of others.

Thomas Henry Huxley

1. Education is learning the rules of the game of life.

2. Time, whose tooth gnaws away everything else, is powerless against truth.

3. The only medicine for suffering, crime, and all the other woes of mankind is wisdom.

4. It is the customary fate of new truths to begin as heresies and to end as superstitions.

5. There is no greater mistake than the hasty conclusion that opinions are worthless because they are badly argued.

6. For every man, the world is as fresh as it was at the first day, and as full of untold novelties for him who has the eyes to see them.

7. Teach a man to read and write, and you have put into his hands the great key of the wisdom box.

8. Plain common sense, as all truth in the long run, is only common sense clarified.

9. The most valuable result of education is the ability to make yourself do the thing you ought to do when it ought to be done, whether you have to do it or not.

10. The rung of a ladder was never meant to rest upon, but only to hold a man's foot long enough to enable him to put the other somewhat higher.

Carl Gustav Jung

1. There is no birth of consciousness without pain.

2. Where love rules, there is no will power; and where power predominates, there love is lacking.

3. A man cannot get rid of himself in favor of an artificial personality without punishment.

4. Never do human beings speculate more, or have more opinions, than about things which they do not understand.

5. We should not pretend to understand the world only by the intellect; we apprehend it just as much by feeling.

6. Every creative man knows that spontaneity is the very essence of creative thought.

7. If a man is capable of leading a responsible life himself, then he is also conscious of his duties to the community.

8. Ultimate truth, if there be such a thing, demands the concert of many voices.

9. Too much of the animal disfigures the civilized human being, too much culture makes a sick animal.

10. Man needs difficulties; they are necessary for health.

Jiddhu Krishnamurti ───────────────────

1. When there's an understanding of the self, then knowledge has its rightful place.

2. Truth is a strange thing; the more you pursue it, the more it will elude you.

3. In listening quietly to the troubles of another, our own burdens are sometimes lightened.

4. Love is an extraordinary thing; without it, life is barren.

5. Life is like a vast river with a great volume of water without a beginning or an ending.

6. Without passion you cannot see the breeze among the leaves or the sunlight on the water.

7. Self-knowledge is the beginning of wisdom in whose tranquillity and silence there is the immeasurable.

8. The mind that is made whole by thought, by knowledge, by experience, is still the result of time and sorrow.

9. Co-operation is possible only when there is freedom from envy, acquisitiveness, and from the craving for personal or collective dominance, power.

10. You may have many possessions and sit in the seat of power, but without beauty and greatness of love, life soon becomes misery and confusion.

James Russell Lowell

1. One thorn of experience is worth a whole wilderness of warning.

2. The foolish and the dead alone never change their opinions.

3. The story of any one man's real experience finds its startling parallel in that of every one of us.

4. Solitude is as needful to the imagination as society is wholesome for the character.

5. Let us be of good cheer remembering that the misfortunes hardest to bear are those which never come.

6. In the scale of the destinies, brawn will never weigh so much as brain.

7. Notoriety may be achieved in a narrow sphere, but fame demands for its evidence a more distant and prolonged reverberation.

8. Things always seem fairer when we look back on them, and it is out of that inaccessible tower of the past that longing leans and beckons.

9. The devil loves nothing better than the intolerance of reformers, and dreads nothing so much as their charity and patience.

10. The only faith that wears well and holds its color in all weathers is that which is woven of conviction and set with the sharp mordant of experience.

Maimonides (Moses ben Maimon) ———————

1. Where words are many and their meaning is small—that is folly.

2. The virtuous life is the moderate life.

3. A man who is captain of his own soul is a greater hero than the commander of hosts.

4. Out of every thousand deaths, one is due to the cruelty of nature; all the others are caused by the stupidity of man.

5. He who toils privately in learning will become wise.

6. I will destroy my enemies by converting them to friends.

7. No joy is greater or more glorious than the joy of gladdening the hearts of the poor, the widows, the orphans and the strangers.

8. Whoever makes vows in order to discipline his moral disposition and to improve his conduct, displays commendable zeal and is worthy of praise.

9. Whoever displays mercy to others will be granted mercy himself.

10. If a man exercises power, his griefs and worries will accumulate.

John Stuart Mill ———————————

1. He who does anything because it is the custom makes no choice.

2. Ask yourself whether you are happy, and you cease to be so.

3. All good things which exist are the fruits of originality.

4. Everyone who received the protection of society owes a return for the benefit.

5. Very few facts are able to tell their own story without comments to bring out their meaning.

6. Whatever crushes individuality is despotism, by whatever name it may be called.

7. All that makes existence valuable to anyone depends on the enforcement of restraints upon the actions of other people.

8. The mental and moral, like the muscular powers, are improved only by being used.

9. Genius can only breathe freely in an atmosphere of freedom.

10. If we were never to act on our opinions, because those opinions may be wrong, we should leave all our interests uncared for, and all our duties unperformed.

Jean Baptiste Molière

1. When love's path runs smoothly it makes life as dull as can be.

2. The proud woman has a heart fit for a queen; the cunning woman is celebrated for her wit, and the fool for her kind nature.

3. The true gentleman is he who never boasts about anything.

4. Nothing is easier when one is rich than to be an honest man; it's when one is poor that it becomes difficult.

5. The greatest weakness of men is their strong attachment to life.

6. There is no reward so delightful, no pleasure so exquisite, as having one's work known and acclaimed by those whose applause confers honor.

7. He who has never been ridiculous is unable to laugh.

8. Teach self-knowledge, which is the height of all wisdom, and knowledge to others, which is the mark of true understanding.

9. The greater the obstacle, the more glory in overcoming it.

10. It is not only what we do, but also what we do not do, for which we are accountable.

George Edward Moore

1. Nature does indeed set limits to what is possible.

2. To act on the results of reflection is hardly ever wise.

3. Pleasure is very valuable as a means to keep us fit for doing other things.

4. There is always a right and a wrong way, and the wrong way always seems the more reasonable.

5. Are not the swinish pleasures more intense?

6. Egoism is undoubtedly superior to altruism as a doctrine of means.

7. One's duty, in any particular situation, is to do that action which will cause more good than any possible alternative.

8. Ethics must decide on what is meant by good.

9. If there be any free will, then it is obviously one of the causes we have to reckon with, in considering how much good is possible.

10. Egoism is the doctrine which holds that we ought each of us to pursue our own greatest happiness as our ultimate end.

Ayn Rand

1. In order to be in control of your life, you have to have a purpose—a productive purpose.

2. When men share the same basic premise, it is the most consistent ones who win.

3. The businessman's tool is values; the bureaucrat's tool is fear.

4. The mark of an honest man is that he means what he says and knows what he means.

5. Whether you know the shape of a pebble or the structure of a solar system, the axioms remain the same: that it exists and that you know it.

6. One's wishes are limited only by the power of one's gang.

7. As man is a being of self-made wealth, so is he a being of self-made soul.

8. When the ablest men turn into cowards, the average men turn into brutes.

9. A morality that holds need as a claim, holds emptiness—non-existence—as its standard of value.

10. A proud man does not negate his own identity.

George Santayana

1. All ambitions must be defeated when they ask for the impossible.

2. What a strange pleasure there is sometimes in seeing what we expect, or hearing what we knew was fact!

3. Man may like to go alone for a walk, but he hates to stand alone in his opinions.

4. The young man who has not wept is a savage, and the old man who will not laugh is a fool.

5. Every passion, like life as a whole, has its feet in one moral climate and its head in another.

6. Perhaps the only true dignity of man is his capacity to despise himself.

7. The heart has reasons of which the reason has no knowledge.

8. Interest in the changing seasons is a much happier state of mind than being hopelessly in love with spring.

9. The great difficulty in education is to get experience out of ideas.

10. A free mind does not measure the worth of anything by the worth of anything else.

Albert Schweitzer

1. It is the fate of every truth to be an object of ridicule when it is first acclaimed.

2. The stronger the reverence for natural life, the stronger grows also that for spiritual life.

3. There is in us an instinctive awe in the presence of life, for we ourselves are sparks of the will to live.

4. The mere setting up of lists of virtues and vices is like vamping on the keyboard and calling the ensuing noise music.

5. Whoever is spared personal pain must feel himself called to help in diminishing the pain of others.

6. The highest knowledge is to know that we are surrounded by mystery.

7. No man is ever completely and permanently a stranger to his fellow man. Man belongs to man.

8. Love is the eternal thing which men can already on earth possess as it really is.

9. We are always walking on loose stones which overhang the precipice of pessimism.

10. The pathway from imperfect to perfect recognized truth leads through the valley of reality.

Lucius Annaeus Seneca

1. Of all felicities, the most charming is that of a firm and gentle friendship.

2. It is a preposterous weakness to love a man before we know him, and not to care for him after.

3. It is not the man who has too little, but the man who craves more, that is poor.

4. You can tell the character of every man when you see how he receives praise.

5. He is most powerful who has power over himself.

6. Eyes will not see when the heart wishes them to be blind.

7. Nothing is so certain as that the evils of idleness can be shaken off by hard work.

8. He who receives a benefit with gratitude repays the first installment on his debt.

9. It is a rough road that leads to the heights of greatness.

10. There is nothing in this world, perhaps, that is talked more of, and less understood, than the business of a happy life.

George Bernard Shaw

1. It's just as unpleasant to get more than you bargain for as to get less.

2. If a person is a born fool, the folly will get worse, not better, by a long life's practice.

3. The test of a man or woman's breeding is how they behave in a quarrel.

4. There are no secrets better kept than the secrets that everybody guesses.

5. The more things a man is ashamed of, the more respectable he is.

6. Silence is the most perfect expression of scorn.

7. The nation's morals are like its teeth: the more decayed they are the more it hurts to touch them.

8. Other people have too many cares of their own to think much about yours.

9. The progress of the world depends on the people who refuse to accept facts and insist on the satisfaction of their instincts.

10. Truth is the one thing nobody will believe.

Voltaire (François-Marie Arouet) _____

1. Let each of us boldly and honestly say: how little it is that I really know!

2. The origin of evil has always been an abyss, the depth of which no one has been able to sound.

3. The progress of rivers to the sea is not as rapid as that of man to error.

4. Man is not born wicked: he becomes so, as he becomes sick.

5. Man has been given everything needed to live in society; just as he has been given a stomach to digest, eyes to see, a soul to judge.

6. The true charter of liberty is independence, maintained by force.

7. It is far better to be silent than merely to increase the quantity of bad books.

8. From generation to generation skepticism increases and probability diminishes; and soon probability is reduced to zero.

9. Liberty is only and can be only the power to do what one wills.

10. Man can have only a certain number of teeth, hair and ideas.

Alfred North Whitehead

1. You cannot postpone your mind's life until you have sharpened it.

2. Knowledge does not keep any better than fish.

3. How the past perishes is how the future becomes.

4. The true difficulty is to understand how anything survives the lapse of time.

5. Nobody who hasn't been knocked down has the slightest notion of what the real is.

6. You can't catch a moment by the scruff of the neck—it's gone, you know.

7. Life is the enjoyment of emotion, derived from the past and aimed at the future.

8. A culture is in its finest flower before it begins to analyze itself.

9. The human body is an instrument for the production of art in the life of the human soul.

10. There is no royal road to learning through an airy path of brilliant generalizations.

Walt Whitman

1. Judging from the main portions of the history of the world so far, justice is always in jeopardy.

2. All faults may be forgiven of him who has perfect candor.

3. With respect to moral virtue or to heroism and religious incumbency, the old principles remain.

4. One is never entirely without the instinct of looking around.

5. Let every man look to himself. Then society will take care of itself.

6. All that a person does or thinks is of consequence.

7. Who should be a better judge of a man's talents than the man himself?

8. I see no reason why we should let our lights shine under bushels.

9. What is humanity in its faith, love, heroism, poetry, even morals, but emotion?

10. To think of all these wonders of city and country, and we take no interest in them.

Oscar Wilde

1. The only thing that one really knows about human nature is that it changes.

2. A man who does not think for himself, does not think at all.

3. If one tells the truth, one is sure, sooner or later, to be found out.

4. To love oneself is the beginning of a life-long romance.

5. That country is the richest which nourishes the greatest number of noble and happy human beings.

6. There is no sin except stupidity.

7. A cynic is a man who knows the price of everything and the value of nothing.

8. Young men want to be faithful, and are not; old men want to be faithless, and cannot.

9. Whenever a man does a thoroughly stupid thing, it is always from the noblest motives.

10. We are all in the gutter, but some of us are looking at the stars.

Index